W... ...t,
in His Light,
Carilyn

Standing Strong in the Power of HIS Might

Relying on Christ's Strength through the Armor of God

Carolyn Pais

ISBN: 1500130281
ISBN 13: 9781500130282

This book is dedicated to Michael, my husband and Rachael, my daughter. I can't help but smile and thank God for the blessing they are to me.

Table of Contents

Acknowledgments

I am so thankful for my wonderful family and friends who have encouraged me through the years. I especially would like to thank everyone who comes to our weekly bible study group. What a blessing you all have been.

For the wonderful photographs that Caitlyn and Justin supplied. When I saw them, I knew they would be the perfect images for the cover of this book. Also, for Johnny and his help fine tuning the cover for me.

For Mike who encouraged me to continue to write and helped edit portions of this book.

For Amy who helped with the final editing. This gave me the confidence that I needed to submit this book to a publisher.

For the editorial evaluation through Createspace that gave such helpful advice for a first time book writer.

Introduction

"Finally, be strong in the Lord and in the power of his might."
Ephesians 6:10 (KJV)

Some of you have read this verse many times. I know I had. Then I asked myself the all-important question when reading God's Word: "Am I living this?" "Am I strong in the Lord and in the power of His might?" My response went something like this: "Well, sort of ..., sometimes, hmm... maybe..." Actually, I came to the conclusion that I wasn't certain if I knew what this verse meant in my everyday life. I also took notice that it's not a suggestion. It's a command.

When I think of being strong in the Lord, I picture the calming of a storm, seeing a lame man walk or driving demons out of possessed people. Further in this study we will see that these powerful acts are still available, but in my typical day; at work, at the grocery store, with friends and family, there's no need for them. This didn't negate the fact that I still felt powerless in many situations. Simple situations, like having the right words to say to someone who obviously needed some encouragement or not saying the wrong words that caused more conflict. Then there's the times where instead of being bitter and accusative when someone hurt my feelings I could have been forgiving and responded lovingly. (Wouldn't that have been refreshing?) As

I mulled over my daily activities it was pretty plain to see that there are many circumstances in which the strength of my Lord and Savior, Jesus Christ, was needed. Some are small, seemingly insignificant, like not losing your patience when driving but then there are those big moments in your life when you see someone in need of deliverance and you grope for some way of helping but you feel so powerless.

It's these situations and others that had made me realize that I needed to learn HOW to "**be strong in the Lord and in the power of his might**" each and every day, moment by moment of my life. My heartfelt desire in writing this book is to show from God's Word how to rely on Christ's strength in extremely practical terms so we all can answer confidently "YES! I am strong in the Lord and in the power of His might!"

One

Empowered in Powerful Power

Finally, be empowered in the Lord and in His powerful power.
(Is God trying to tell us something here?)

The King James Version of the bible translates Ephesians 6:10 as **"Finally, be strong in the Lord and the power of his might."** The words **"strong," "power"** and **"might"** in the original Greek as well as in English are synonymous words. Even though in the Greek they are different very often these same words are translated **"power."** When studying them I realized that it could have been translated as I did in this chapter heading. "Finally, be empowered in the Lord and in His powerful power." Knowing this, would you say God was trying to emphasize a point? God wants us to be powerful! Our heavenly Father wants us to be empowered with the powerful power of our Lord Jesus Christ.

Now each of these words describes a different aspect of power. In our quest to rely on this power it is important to understand the subtle nuances of these words by looking at the Greek they were translated from. Let's start with **"strong."**

1

"Strong"
Endunamoo

The word "**strong**" is the Greek word *endunamoo*, which is from the root word *dunamis*. We get the English words dynamo, dynamic and dynamite from this Greek word. In essence it means innate ability. It is the source from which we can do things. The definition of the word dynamo helped me to understand it even better.

Dynamo - 1. A generator, esp. one that produces direct current. (Webster's II New College Dictionary)

One winter, New England and Eastern Canada had severe ice storms. Much of that area was without power. I called my brother who lives in Vermont to see how he and his family were doing. My brother being a wilderness type of guy responded "Fine. Why do you ask?" I began to explain what I saw on the weather station but guessed that stormed missed Winooski, Vermont. He said, "No, the whole area is without power except those people who had generators." Of course, he rented a generator (and had everything else needed to make it through major ice or snow storms.) He explained to me how as soon as the outside power failed they put the generator to use. It became the power source for their home. The only problem with their generator was it had limited power so they had to be selective with what they used it for (i.e., not a good time to leave all the lights on in the house.)

Think for a moment how you have a "spiritual generator" within. It's a source of power ready to be used at any time. That "spiritual generator," that "dynamo" has a name. His name is Jesus Christ. He is the source of the power that enables us to do all things that are needed to represent Him in our day and time.

The great news is that contrary to a generator, Christ's power within is limitless. It can never be used up. In II Corinthians, chapter 12, Paul describes a particular hard situation that he was in. The answer to his prayer for help that our Lord gave him in verse 9 was: "**My grace is sufficient for you, for my power [*dunamis*] is made perfect in weakness.**" When we recognize that we are weak in our own power, abilities and resources that is when Christ's power can work. When we hear ourselves say (or think) things like "I can't handle this!" "You owe me!" "I'd like to slap you upside the head!" "I'm so confused - I don't know how to handle this." (I'm sure we could come up with many more examples.) These are clear indications our power is out and we need to "plug" into the ultimate power source, Jesus Christ. Since it is unlimited we don't need to be selective like only in the above-mentioned, nerve-racking moments. Jesus wants us "plugged in," shining bright at all times!

To further send this point home notice what Philippians 4:13 says. "**I can do everything through him who gives me strength [*endunamoo*].**" My brother could weather a severe ice storm with the aid of a small rented generator. What about the "storms" that come our way? The command "**be strong**" in Ephesians 6:10 simply means: allow Jesus Christ to empower you by staying connected, "plugged in" to Him. This brings us to the next word in this study... "**And.**"

⌒

"And"

Such a simple word that could easily be overlooked, but it's there for a reason. Yes, we are to be strong, empowered, in Christ Jesus our Lord "**and in the power of his might.**" There's a next level to this strength! More than just empowered in our everyday lives to stand strong, God wants us to be a force that is to be reckoned with. Yes, we can be patient and we also can move mountains (see: Matthew 17:20). That takes some spiritual muscle power! When our alarms go off, Satan and his demonic accomplices should be "alarmed." We have more power in us through Christ than all the evil forces combined. 1 John 4:4 confirms this: **"… greater is he that is in you, than he that is in the world."** We'll also see this as we study the next two words **"power"** [*kratos*] and **"might"** [*iskus*].

"Power"
Kratos

Kratos is typically translated **"power"** but in the King James Version it is also translated "dominion" (I Peter 4:11, 5:11, Jude 25 and Revelation 1:6). The word "dominion" gives us more of the flavor of the word. It means to dominate, to rule or control by superior power or force. In Ephesians 1:18-20, Paul prays for us to know by experience this power and gives us an eye opening description of the force of this power.

"… that you may know… what is the exceeding greatness of His power to us-ward who believe, according to the working of His mighty power [*kratos*] which He wrought in Christ when He raised Him from the dead and set Him at His own right hand in the heavenly *places*."

This **"power"** is what God used to raise Jesus from the dead. That's extreme power. God didn't just breathe life into Jesus' body but He gave Jesus a resurrected, spiritual body and set Him at His own right hand **"and God placed all things under his feet and appointed him to be the head over everything for the church,"** (Eph. 1:22). Is this not the ultimate example of superior power? God could do this because He's God! He is the creator of the universe! He is all-powerful! What He says goes! What's really wild is that this type of power is available to us! As His children He wants us to realize that we have supernatural power and that we are placed in a position where we also can and should rule. Romans 5:17 says, "... **how much more will those who receive God's abundant provision of grace and of the gift of righteousness reign in life through one man, Jesus Christ.**" To "**reign in life**" is to rule! It's through Jesus Christ we receive this authority and power. He wants us to reign. If you are reigning in life you are on top, dominating your opponents as well as exerting mastery over your own passions and desires. Of course to dominate you need muscle power, which is exactly what the next word of our study is: "**might.**"

"Might"
Iskus

Iskus is usually translated "**might,**" "**strength**" or "**power.**" In Matthews 12:29 we see the adjective form, *iskuros,* "**strong**" man indicating this man had some muscles and was not to be messed with (unless you tied him up good!) Think of what muscle bound men can do. I've seen them lift up cars! In Matthew 14:30 the boisterous [*iskuros*] wind scared Peter while he was walking on the water towards Jesus. It was obviously intimidating! We recently had part of our roof blown off by a strong, very intimidating wind. It gave me a new understanding of the word, might. A force not to mess with!

Most of us watched or read about super heroes who were mighty and could do great exploits because of their superior strength and abilities. Well, you've got what it takes to be a super hero! "...the power of **his might.**" Hello! That's true super hero power!

"Power of His Might"

When we look at both Greek words *kratos* and *iskus* it's obvious that this "**power**" is fighting power, ruling power, as well as, transforming power. It is extreme strength used to dominate our foes as well as bring about **"God's good and pleasing and perfect will."** (See Romans 12:2) We are to be empowered in the Lord and use His might to dominate the spiritual forces so that good prevails!

"Finally, be strong in the Lord and in the power of his might."

To sum up this chapter I'd like to propose a balanced perspective. I've seen many Christians take this verse and use it only when times were hard. Of course, that's a large part of when we rely on this power. It is certainly to be used during "storms" in our lives. But these same believers fail to take seriously what Jesus said. **"I tell you the truth, anyone who has faith in me will do what I have been doing. He will do even greater things than these, because I am going to the Father."** (John 14:12) Notice Jesus said **"anyone who has faith me"**. First question: Do you have faith in Jesus Christ? Secondly, what did Jesus do? Let's see... He healed the sick, cast out demons, performed miracles... By not believing this verse, many Christians miss out on the **"ruling, mighty power"** we now have because Jesus Christ fulfilled this verse and now **"sits at the right hand of God...and appointed him to be head over everything for the church."** (Eph. 1:20, 22) We have the power to do what Jesus did. That's what this "**power of his might**" is all about.

Then there's the other side of the scale: Christians who started off with great zeal to serve God. They were leading worldwide ministries, healing the sick, performing miracles, teaching powerful messages... and then they fall! Why? It was because they failed to use the power in their everyday lives. They did not **"by the Spirit... put to death the misdeeds of the body..."** (Romans 8:13) but rather allowed a temptation to lead them into sins, which destroyed their ministries. They too, didn't take John 14:12 seriously. Jesus Christ also walked in wisdom and said no to temptations. We too have the power to say no. We are commanded to be **"strong** (empowered) **in the Lord"** to live pure, holy lives.

The balanced perspective is to be **"strong,"** standing firm during trials, resisting temptations **"and"** use **"the power of his might"** as an opposing force against our enemies, doing what Jesus did when He walked the earth. As you probably noticed the power is both for the defense and the offense. That's what armor is all about. In the verses that follow Ephesians 6:10 we will see why being **"strong in the Lord and the power of his might"** is absolutely essential to victorious Christian living. If you haven't noticed yet we are in a battle and we need to **"put on the whole armor of God!"**

Two

We're in a Battle!

Yes, we're in a battle! We live in a war zone! We get a clear picture of who our real enemy is in the next three verses in Ephesians.

"Put on the full armor of God so that you can take your stand against the devil's schemes. For our struggle is not against flesh and blood, but against the rulers, against the authorities, against the powers of this dark world and against the spiritual forces of evil in the heavenly realms. Therefore put on the full armor of God, so that when the day of evil comes, you may be able to stand your ground, and after you done every-thing, to stand." Ephesians 6:11-13

Good vs. Evil

These three verses give us the answer to the question "Why is there so much pain and suffering in the world?" We are in a spiritual battle. Whether you are Christian or not, you are still affected by this battle. There are "bombs" exploding in many places in our world literally as well as figuratively. The **"devil's schemes"** include real artillery as well as other destructive forces that steal from and kill innocent people. Sometimes they occur quickly, like through a drunken driver or slowly, like an addiction to drugs or an illness like cancer. Many Christians numbly watch and assume it must be God's will. They are ambushed daily and letting the enemy take them as prisoners of war almost willingly. Jesus, in John 10:10 clearly tells us the difference between what the devil's up to and what He, Jesus, wants for our lives. **"The thief comes only to steal and kill and destroy; I have come that they may have life and have it to the full."** It's pretty plain to see the stark difference. So, if what is going on in your life, or others, is under the categories of stealing, killing and destroying, please, don't call it God's will! Jesus Christ came to fulfill God's will and that is for us to be able to have **"full"** lives! Lives full of purpose, peace, joy, love and everything else that represents God's goodness. That is why we have the **"full armor of God"** to protect us against the stealer, the killer and the destroyer!

Two other verses that are very explicit in describing what the devil is up to are in I Peter 5:8-9:

"Be self-controlled and alert. Your enemy the devil prowls around as a roaring lion looking for someone to devour. Resist him, standing firm in the faith, because you know that your brothers throughout the world are undergoing the same kind of sufferings."

It's extremely important for us to understand that the sufferings that many of us are going through are not from God but come from the devil who is prowling around devouring some and leaving "bite marks" on many. The good news is that God has provided a way for us to beat the devil even here. He can use our suffering for good. In Romans 5:3-4, God tells us to "...**rejoice in our sufferings because we know that sufferings produce**

perseverance, perseverance, character; and character, hope."
Of course, if you don't persevere (which means to remain standing for God while under pressure) you can forget having character (proven integrity) and life gets pretty hopeless. But… if you
do persevere, building proven integrity, you become a hopeful,
joyous person. You've then squashed another demonic scheme!
Also, in the midst of trials we have the opportunity to see Christ
strength working in us (II Corinthians 12:9). We would never
experience this if every difficulty had a quick fix. Sometimes
God's answer to our prayers is for us to rely on Christ's strength.

The key is to realize we are living in a fallen world in which
the devil and his demonic forces are busy rousing up evil. God
makes it plain in His Word that there will be suffering, but also
that He has made a way out. It's through believing in His Son,
Jesus Christ, who is **"the way"**. (John 14:6) For those of us who
believe in the death and resurrection of Jesus Christ and have
made Jesus their Lord (hopefully everyone reading this book)
have eternal life. (See Romans 10:9, 10) We have the hope of a
new heaven and earth where Satan and his evil forces have no
place. That was God's desire in the first place with the Garden of
Eden. The only thing that could cause a problem was…freedom
of will.

Freedom of Will

If God hadn't given humans and angels the freedom of will to
choose to love Him the world would still be perfect… except for
the "robot like" humans and angels! Think of what it would feel
like to be with someone who had no choice but to act "loving" towards you. They would actually not be loving you. What makes
true love so special is that it's by choice! When asked what the
greatest commandment was, Jesus said, **"Love the Lord your**

God with all your heart and with all your soul and with all your mind."(Matt. 27:37) If our hearts, souls and minds were created to automatically do this than God wouldn't have to ask us to. Obedience to this command is a choice.

So is …rebellion.

Satan chose to rebel (Read Isaiah 14:12-14) He had been called **"the morning star, son of the dawn"** but decided he wanted to be **"above"** God. Many theologians agree that Revelation 12:3 implies that as many as one third of the angels were cast out of heaven with him. They have been influencing mankind to also rebel against God and do hideous things. The holocaust, slavery, drug marketing, child pornography, the sex trade, terrorism are just of few of the horrendous acts of evil that have caused incredible suffering throughout all the ages.

They have also influenced some of us to do stupid things that have also caused a lot of trouble and grief. Some of which are: becoming addicted to alcohol, drugs or gambling, refusing to forgive, putting others down, affairs...

The choices we make are ours but the influences can be very subtle. One wrong choice and the next thing you know you are in a dilemma! Of course, this is part of the **"devil's schemes"** and why the next chapter is about being aware of them.

Three

Other Ways

There are other ways, but do they take us where we want to go?

First of all, it's important to notice that we are to "**put on the full armor of God so that you can take your stand against the devil's schemes.**" Phew! You can wipe the sweat off your brow. It's not about you being so smart but about putting on "**the armor!**" It's about what we are "wearing"... mentally! We've been given the "**armor of God**" but like any gift it's our part to put it on which takes using our minds. Thinking what God's word says. Having our minds sharpened by God's word is essential to noticing the "**devil's schemes.**" The Greek word that's translated "**schemes**" here is *methodos*, which is where we get our English word method - a way to do something.

Methodos is made up from two words: *meta* which simply means **with** and *odos* which is usually translated "**way,**" "**journey,**" or "**road.**" Remember, Jesus Christ said, "**I am the way** [*odos*] **and the truth and the life.**"(John 14:6) Well, the devil has "ways" he uses to lure us away from following Christ "**the truth and the life.**" He tempts us with other roads to take. Lies that lead to death! Let's take a look at some of them.

Big Babies!

The most prevalent way to keep Christians from truly follow-ing Christ is to keep them in their "play pens". The expres-sion "You're acting like a big baby!" fits so many Christians. How does Satan do it? He does it by keeping us from knowing the truth which is what we need to fully mature in Christ. To grow up and be like Christ we need to know Him. Ephesians 4:11-15 tells us that Jesus appointed some in the church to be apostles, prophets, evangelists, pastors and teachers. All those ministries have one thing in common; they have to use their mouths to speak the truth. Their purpose is **"to prepare God's people for works of service so that the body of Christ may be built up until we all reach unity in the faith and in the knowl-edge of the Son of God and become mature attaining to the whole measure of the fullness of Christ. Then we will no lon-ger be infants..."** It then says what happens to infants in the church, they are pushed around by **"deceitful scheming."** One of Satan's biggest schemes is to keep us away from people who can help us learn the truth and mature, as well as, encourage us to stay on the path of truth.

Our main purpose as members in the body of Christ is to help each other live the truth. Verse 15 says. **"Instead,"** (instead of being big babies!) **"speaking the truth in love we will in all things grow up into him who is the Head, that is, Christ."** The Greek for **"speaking the truth."** is one word, *aletheuo.* It means to not only speak the truth but to live the truth; the truth ultimately being God's Word. Jesus prayed: **"Sanctify them by the truth, thy word is truth."** (John 17:17) Knowing and living the truth is how we grow up and keep from falling into trouble by Satan's deceitful scheming. This is being sanctified, set apart from sin and it's consequences as we live the truth for God like Jesus did. With all this in mind, what do you think our very first piece of armor is? **"The belt of truth!"**

It's pretty obvious that the Devil's most prevalent scheme is to keep people from knowing the truth. Once people know some of the truth he has to come up with other ways to either steal the truth they learned or keep them from truly living it. Jesus explained how this is done when He told His disciples the meaning of the **"parable of the sower"** in Matthew 13:18-23.

Ways Satan Deals with Truth

First Method: Snatches it Away

The first method Satan uses is to try stealing the truth from us is when we first hear it and we haven't quite understood it. Verse 19: **"When anyone hears the message about the kingdom and does not understand it, the evil one snatches away what was sown in his heart. This is the seed sown along the path."** So often someone will hear the message of salvation and becoming a child of God and they get excited but they really haven't processed it enough to believe. We in the church have to remember these people are targets for Satan to steal whatever they have heard. How does he steal? Very often it could be by placing a doubt that whatever they heard was too good to be true. Another tactic is the realization that things they believed to be true go against what God's Word says. This can be hard for some people to accept. We are to be alert to this scheme. We can help them through prayer and continuing to lovingly share the truth with them. Remember part of our job is to help others grow. Following up and helping others understand is one way to "slap the evil one's hand" as he tries to snatch!

Second Method: Beats it Out of You:

The next way Jesus described is in verses 20 and 21: **"The one who received the seed that fell on rocky places is the man who hears the word and at once receives it with joy. But since he has no root, he lasts only a short time. When trouble or persecution comes because of the word, he quickly falls away."** This is like the person who got all excited when they heard about Jesus and how He gave His life for them. They'd go to church or listen to a friend about what is available in Christ but never did study the bible or put into practice what they had heard. Then trouble comes... Remember the Devil is the biggest troublemaker! He's a master at stealing, killing and destroying. Instead of asking Jesus for help they fall back to the old ways they dealt with pain: drinking or drugs, lashing out, depression...

If our adversary doesn't cause **"trouble,"** then he will endeavor to bring **"persecution."** Satan could send others to ridicule them for their new beliefs. Often it's "friends" or family members who tell them in no uncertain terms that they are either really stupid for believing the bible or in some places they are threatened with real persecution (imprisonment or death) for becoming a Christian. At this point they have to make a decision and without really knowing the power that's available they give up their pursuit of knowing Jesus.

There's a reason that Jesus shared these methods of how the truth gets taken away. It's not hard to notice when a new believer is in trouble or being persecuted. When we see these warning signs we really need to come by their side and fight for them. We also need to speak the truth that will encourage them to keep their faith. Later on in this book we will see in greater detail how we are equipped with ammunition to help defeat this evil scheme.

Method Three: Chokes it Out of You

The next scenario in verse 22 is where many of us Christians exist. **"The one who receives the seed that fell among the thorns is the man who hears the word, but the worries of this life and the deceitfulness of wealth choke it, making it unfruitful."** In fact, this scheme works two ways! One way is that it keeps others from wanting to become Christians because they don't see any difference between Christians and the rest of the world. What they do see is hypocrisy. They hear many of us talking about love, joy, peace… but they don't see any of that in our lives. Why? Because these Christians are too busy worrying or being greedy.

Worry, I know this is where I've struggled. It's so easy. It's so useless! It is also something we are commanded not to do but, our minds can slip into the worry mode of the "What ifs…?" Thankfully we don't have to allow ourselves to be choked by this! As we will see, we can choose what to think!

Then the other thorn that chokes is greed: continuing to want more money or material possessions. This is so tempting! Any television commercial, newspaper ad or your friend's new shoes can do this! We can overcome these temptations by choosing the fruitful way to live.

Overcoming Satan's Methods: The Fruitful Way to Live

Verse 23 describes the best way to live: **"But the one received the seed that fell on good soil is the man who hears the word and understands it. He produces a crop, yielding a hundred, sixty or thirty times what was sown."** That's fruitful living! Fruit meaning good results, acts of kindness, peaceful hearts, joyful countenances, generosity... When people see this kind of fruit they will want it too and that produces the greatest fruit of all - others coming to Jesus and receiving eternal life!

It's important to realize that we need to **"take our stand against the devil's schemes"** by making it a point to learn, understand and apply the truth. Satan will do all he can to keep us from knowing Jesus and living for Him. There are so many distractions, so many different temptations that try to lure us away from Christ out there! It's a relief to know that we have **"the full armor of God"** to put on so we can take our stand. The armor is our protection as well as our weapon against the evil forces.

Four

Who are we fighting, anyway?

"For our struggle is not against flesh and blood, but against the rulers, against the authorities, against the powers of this dark world and against the spiritual forces of evil in the heavenly realms."
Ephesians 6:12

No matter how it seems that our struggles are with people or even ourselves the truth is our struggles are influenced by evil forces. These forces thrive on the sin nature of man, such as pride, lust, prejudice, bitterness, hatred… Even illnesses, although they take place in our bodies the above verse tells us that they do not stem from a flesh and blood matter. This doesn't mean that every sickness is a direct consequence of a person's sin or that they've been affected by a demon. Many of the illnesses that affect people have come through poisons that infiltrate our water, food and air. It's important to recognize that illnesses are not God's will for mankind. They are part of the stealing, killing and destroying agenda of Satan. We are fighting against evil forces. You might be asking: Who or what are they? That's a good question! Let's start with whose overall in charge of these evil forces.

19

The Ultimate Control Freak

I John 5:19 says, **"the whole world is under the control of the evil one."** II Corinthians 4:4 states **"The god of this age has blinded the minds of unbelievers, so that they cannot see the light of the gospel of the glory of Christ, who is the image of God."** It is interesting to note that God gave us freedom of will but Satan is all about control. Some of you might have heard someone jokingly say "the devil made me do it." Well, without knowledge of the truth, blinded to the light of the gospel, people are being led around, controlled by Satan.

Besides people, demons are also under his control. In Matthew 9:43 he is referred to as the **"prince of demons."** Jesus called him **"the prince of this world"** in John 12:31. In Ephesians 2:2 he is called **"the ruler of the kingdom of the air."** He is ultimately in charge but he has a lot of help implementing his evil schemes. It's obvious in Ephesians 6:12 that he has set up a hierarchy of power starting with **"rulers."**

Rulers

"Rulers" is translated from the Greek word *arche.* This was the title for the highest dignitaries of the state. In Satan's kingdom, it's the demons he's put in charge of specific regions or even possibly specific influences.

In the Daniel 10:12-13 we see an example of this, a particular ruler that withstood an angel sent by God. **"...your words were heard and I have come in response to them. But** the prince of the Persian kingdom resisted me twenty-one days then Michael, one of the chief princes, came to help me, because I was detained there with the king of Persia."

Michael, the archangel, (arch is also from the Greek word *arche*) had to come help another angel fight off this **"prince,"** ruler of the Persian kingdom. I'd say this ruler is seriously strong but then again this gives us more reasons to pray because both angels came in response to a prayer!

Authorities

"Authorities" (*exousia* in Greek) implies the ability to make ones power felt. It's like a manager of a department of a corporation. The workers follow the manager's orders but the orders are in line with the corporate goals, which in this case is **"to steal, to kill and to destroy"** (back to John 10:10!) Of course, our Lord Jesus has given us authority. We are to make His power felt over any evil forces by helping others live the full and eternal life He came to bring!

Powers of this Dark World

"Powers" is translated from a compound Greek word *kosmokrator.* (Already sounds intimidating!) *Kosmos* is usually translated "world" which is in light of its order and design. *Krator* is translated "take by the hand," "lay hold of" or "hold fast." The word **"world"** in this verse is *aion* and signifies duration of time as in, these days or this age. These **"powers"** have specific qualities. They operate in a deliberate, methodical order and have strong grips. It's obvious to see their effects over the ages. They systematically lead people one step at a time into darkness through addictions, greed, pride, vanity, ignorance... It's of utmost importance for us to realize that we too need to be deliberate as we **"hold firmly [*krator*] to the faith we profess."** (Hebrews 4:14)

⟜⟶

Spiritual Forces of Evil in the Heavenly Realms

"Forces of evil," *poneria* in the Greek, is the full realm of evil in every aspect. It's also translated **"wickedness"** (KJV). These spirits main job is to instill diabolical thinking. They are the instigators of the insane, sick, creepy thoughts and actions that make headline news regularly. If you ever wondered how people can get so wicked, well they have lots of help!

I hope you are realizing how serious it is for us to wear our spiritual armor. Ephesians 5:15 says: **"Be very careful, then how you live - not as unwise but as wise, making the most of every opportunity, because the days are evil [*ponero*]."** We live in wicked, evil times but we can make the most of every opportunity by using our spiritual armor.

We need to be **"strong in the Lord and in His mighty power"** not only for our benefit but because the world needs to see the light of Christ. Besides dispelling darkness we also get to be part of another plan. In Ephesians 3:10 we see that God's plan is to let these evil forces know He's wise to their schemes through us. **"His intent was that now, through the church, the manifold wisdom of God should be made known to the rulers and authorities in the heavenly realms."**

So, are you ready to dispel darkness and shine bright, helping others to know Christ's love for them? Are you ready to be a force for good? Are you ready to be **"strong in the Lord and in His mighty power?"** I hope so cause we are all needed and the armor is ours to wear!

Five

How Do You Put on God's Armor?

We can know what each piece of armor is. Have many scripture verses memorized. We can be real Bible scholars and still fall victim to Satan's abuse. Why? The reason is we hadn't put on some or all of our armor. Putting something on takes deliberate actions. Most of us women know this. We'll stand staring at our clothes, thinking through what kind of impression we'd like to make: formal, casual, attractive (of course), fun or just plan comfortable. When it comes to putting on the armor of God, it also takes a decision process.

Ephesians 6:13 starts out with the word "**therefore**" which reminds me to ask the question: what is the "**therefore**" there for? This brings us back to the "**spiritual forces**" that are out to get us. They aren't stupid. They know when we are dressed for battle and when we are wearing old, smelly, hand me downs or simply empty headed - naked!

"Therefore put on the full armor of God so that when the day of evil comes you may be able to stand your ground..."

Okay, so how do you put this armor that comes from God on?

This is probably the most crucial point in the book. It's not just about knowing what this armor that God has given us is, but about truly wearing it. It's time to look at this in practical terms. How do you **"put on"** something that's spiritual? Ephesians 4:22-24 gives us a good start in understanding this concept:

"You were taught, with regard to your former way of life, to put off your old self, which is being corrupted by its deceitful desires; to be made new in the attitude of you minds; and put on the new self, created to be like God in true righteousness and holiness."

"Be made new in the attitude of your minds." Here's another way of saying this. Become the new you by changing your attitude, the way you think about things. **"The new self"** is who you are in Christ. It's the righteous and holy self that God created. Romans 12:2 Is even more explicit. **"... be transformed by the renewing of your mind. Then you will be able to test and approve what God's will is - his good, pleasing and perfect will."**

Transformed!

"Be Transformed." Yes, it's available! You can change... super hero style! The Greek word translated **"transformed"** is *metamorphoomai.* It's where we get our English word metamorphosis: a physical change in form. One vivid example of this is the caterpillar to a butterfly: from a somewhat ugly, crawling on the ground, critter to a majestic, flying, work of art. Of course, there's the example of Superman, from an everyday guy to "The Man of Steel." The point is we too can **"be transformed"** and God's Word tells us how.

The Renewed Mind

When you look up the word **"renewing"** you'll find it means to renovate, to make other and different from that which had been formerly. I totally get this. In fact, for the past week my husband, our friend Mike and I have been ripping out old, dirty and in some places smelly carpet. We are replacing it with wood flooring. To renew our minds is to get rid of the old, dirty and sometimes smelly thoughts and replace them with new, wholesome, clean thoughts. Where can we find these thoughts? God's Word! His Word tells us what to think about regarding any given situation or person (including ourselves). Thinking the right thoughts leads to doing the right things. It's as simple as that. Now it might be simple, but it's not always easy. Remember we have an enemy who is always trying to get us on the wrong path, by feeding us the wrong thoughts about ourselves, others and life in general.

It's Time for Demolition!

The point is we can decide what to think. I Corinthians 10:5 puts it this way: **"We demolish arguments and every pretension that sets itself up against the knowledge of God and we take captive every thought to make it obedient to Christ."** Okay, how's that for putting it in perspective! You can control what you think. You can rip out disgusting, false, wimpy, anxious, prideful - wrong thoughts. God created our brains with that ability. If you have thoughts that do not agree with what God says, get rid of them.

Remember, to renovate means you replace, change what was previously. Once we notice a wrong thought, we need to replace it quickly with the truth. We can say, "You don't belong in my brain. I have decided to think what Christ would have me think!" That's what we need to do with those wrong thoughts we are leading captive. We kick them out and put right ones in their place. We do not have to allow our thoughts to captivate us but we can decide to think what's true and follow Christ.

Jesus told us that it's the truth that will set us free. (John 8:32) This renovation is like taking a prison, our old self, and turning it into "home sweet home" where Jesus lives, our new self.

When I look at my new floors I can't help but smile. I'm not seeing stains or smelling cat pee. The results are pleasing. Well, when we renew our minds, renovate our thinking, the results are really pleasing because we get to **"test and approve what God's will is - his good, pleasing and perfect will."** (Romans 12:2)

So, **"to put on"** means to think what God's Word says and live it out. Again, it's important to realize, that it takes a conscious effort. Like ripping out old carpet, it's not easy, simple, but not easy. Remember we have an enemy whose major goal is to keep us out of our armor. When we are ready for battle we not only protect ourselves but we can effectively ambush his schemes. I'm sure you're like me and want to be a contender for good in this battle. Well, it starts with knowing the truth, God's Word. Our very first piece of armor that you'll need to have on tight is the **"belt of truth."**

Six

The Belt of Truth

**"Stand firm then, with the belt of truth
buckled around your waist…"**
Ephesians 6:14a

A **"belt?"** When I think of armor, a belt isn't part of my mental picture. But, once you study what the roman soldiers wore you realize how important the belt was. It had a twofold purpose. The first is to protect the loin area, the lumbar region of the back, which consists of five vertebrae. These are the largest and strongest in the spinal column. Anyone who does physical work or lifts weights knows (or should know) to protect this area. An injury to this area is not only excruciating but very debilitating. This is why today's trainers and physical therapists put a strong emphasis on the core (the modern name for the loin area). They recognize that a healthy core is foundational to the rest of the body being able to function optimally.

The other function of the soldier's belt was that it served to hold most of the other pieces of the armor in place. The breastplate, shield and sword were all attached to the belt. We will see how necessary it is to first put on **"the belt of truth"** for protection as well as to enable us to carry and use the other armor.

⌐‿⌐

What is Truth?

In John 18:37 Jesus explained to Pilate, the roman governor, right before his crucifixion **"for this reason I was born, and for this I came into the world, to testify to the truth. Everyone on the side of truth listens to me."** Verse 38: **"What is truth? Pilate asked."**

I'm not sure if Pilate asked this question wanting to know an answer or if he was ambivalent because just like today there were so many different belief systems claiming to be the truth. Either way, it's a seriously important question. Of course, one of Satan's methods is to keep people from even asking this question. Then if they do, he's got many other ways that he will point them to that lay claim to being the truth. Jesus said He came into the world to **"testify to the truth."** The simple fact is to really know the truth we need to listen to Jesus! He alone is **"… the way and the truth and the life."** John 14:6

One way to answer the question **"What is truth?"** is to understand that it's the opposite of a lie or what is false. Think of a true or false test. There's no in between. Either you check true or false. We are tested everyday to check off true or false, right or wrong, by how we decide to live. II Corinthians 13:5 says it very plainly: **"Examine yourselves to see whether you are in the faith; test yourselves. Do you not realize that Christ Jesus is in you - unless of course you fail the test?"** Verse 8 shows what A+ students look like. **"For we cannot do anything against the truth, but only for the truth."**

The good news about this test is it's an open book test. This means we need to open the book, God's Word, and live by it. In John 17:17 Jesus prayed that we would be **"sanctified** [set apart] **by the truth, your word is truth."** **"Word"** here is the Greek word *logos*, which means the revealed will of God. To live by the truth is to live our lives according to God's will for our lives.

⌒

The Opposite of Living the Truth

On the other hand, Jesus explained very clearly what the devil is all about: **"… there is no truth in him, when he lies, he speaks his own native language, for he is a liar and the father of lies."** (John 8:44) Obviously, his will is for all of us to live out the false answers. He wants all of us to fail! How often have people looked back at their lives and realized that they had lived it all wrong. That they believed his lies and missed out on what was truly good.

Before we go any further I do want to point out another word that is also translated **"word"** which is *rhema*. Later on we will study the **"sword of the spirit which is the word [*rhema*] of God"**. *Rhema* often refers to specific verses for specific attacks which we will see also helps us from living the lies Satan influences us with. On the other hand, the **"belt of truth"** is committing ourselves to obey God's Word in our everyday lives. To make it a habit to study it, so we can know it, think it and can live it out.

⌒

Where to start?

This might seem very intimidating to some. The Bible is a pretty big book. You might be asking: "Where do I start?" One simple way to begin is by reading the letters written to the church that follow the book of Acts. These were all written after the resurrection of our Lord Jesus Christ and reveal to us what we now have as followers of Christ. They also tell us how we should live as members of the body of Christ, His church. Basic truths that when lived, enable us to shine bright in a dark world.

For example, in Colossians 3:5-9, we are told to **"put to death, therefore, whatever belongs to your earthly nature: sexual immorality, impurity, lust, evil desires and greed...rage, malice, slander, filthy language,.. Do not lie..."** Then in verses 12-14 we are told **"as God's chosen people, holy and dearly loved, clothed yourselves with compassion, kindness, humility, gentleness and patience ... forgive as the Lord forgave you, and over all these virtues put on love..."**

Okay, just looking at these two natures that people exhibit. Who would you rather hang out with, those who live according to their earthly nature or those who are following Christ's example? By the way, since you get to be with yourself all the time choosing to obey God's will is a huge plus for you too!

It's our choice to embrace these virtues. Compassion, kindness, humility, gentleness, patience, forgiveness and the one that covers them all, love. If God says we can wear these virtues - we can! The devil is crafty and will try to talk you out of your potential as one of **"God's chosen people, holy and dearly loved..."** Remember, he's a liar!

Easy Prey

Another important factor is that when our lives are not based on truth we are easy prey for Satan. Think about it. If someone is doing something that is opposite of what God says to do (like having an affair, getting drunk, cheating on tests, stealing, gossiping, etc.) the end results are not good! You do reap what you sow (Galatians 6:7). Actually you are doing exactly what Satan wants you to do which will result is some form of pain. Yes, God does supply mercy, but we still experience the hardship from wrong decisions. If we decide to be ethical, loving, kind, hard workers, say no to drugs and heavy drinking, as well as all the other good things God tells us to do, life stays a lot simpler. Blessings follow obedience as faithfully as consequences follow disobedience. James 1:25 clearly states: **"But the man who looks intently into the perfect law that gives freedom, and continues to do this, not forgetting what he has heard, but doing it - he will be blessed in what he does."** The key to not being easy prey but instead have lives that are blessed is to not forget to do what God says to do.

Benefits from Wearing Our Belt of Truth

Here are a few verses (there are many more) that tell us how beneficial it is to know and live God's Word, which is having our **"belt of truth"** in place.

John 8:31, 32 The truth allows us to be free.

II Timothy 2:16 It equips us for every good work.

James 1:25 We are blessed.

I John 2:3 We get to know God intimately.

II Peter 1:2 We receive grace and peace.

II Peter 1:3 We have everything we need for life and godliness.

II Peter 1:4 It's our escape route from the corruption of the world.

Hebrews 4:12 It's alive and active. The spoken word is powerful!

Romans 12:2 It has the power to transform us.

Ephesians 6:10 Needless to say... It's our armor!

The key here is to know what God's Word says and take it serious. So often we allow ourselves to be tricked into believing it's okay to not obey the truth in certain circumstances because well... "We're only human." But, guess what? The truth is we are more than just human. As a Christian you now have the Holy Spirit dwelling in you. We can do all things through Christ who strengthens us! (Philippians 4:13) We really have no excuses. As you study God's word you will find out that He has given us help through His spirit. Christ's strength is real and works through us so that we can live the truth.

Exam Time

Everyday is an exam. Are you being compassionate, kind, patient... basically living out the truth in the different circumstances of your life? Remember we are told to **"Examine yourselves... test yourselves."** That means: look at what you are doing - which usually starts with what you are thinking. Ask yourself if it's right. Is it what God's Word says to do? If not, ask for help. Hebrews 4:15-16 tells us that Jesus can sympathize with our weaknesses and wants to help us. Some of you might remember the WWJD bracelets that were used as a reminder to ask - What would Jesus do? It's still a great question to ask and He wants to answer and help you do it His way.

We are commanded to put the belt of truth on every morning as we step out of bed and into our everyday life. It is not a burden - it's a necessity. We can stand strong and show people what a sanctified, set-apart-by-truth life looks like. In this day and time people need to see it. They need to see the truth lived out. They need to see the joy, the love, the peace... that's available when we live the truth. Of course, we need it too. So, cinch that belt on tight so that our next piece of armor can stay in place: "**The breastplate of righteousness**."

Seven

The Breastplate of Righteousness

"Stand firm …with the breastplate of righteousness in place."

Picture in your mind a roman soldier. What piece of armor do you see? Many of you probably saw the breastplate. It was made of metal, usually iron, bronze or brass. It covered the torso, both front and back. Also, because it was made of metal, it reflected light - it shined. If you were the only one in a crowd wearing one - you stood out! It was obvious you were a soldier and who your allegiance was to.

The breastplate like the belt had more than one purpose. The obvious one was for protecting the vital organs, especially the heart. But it also was a piece of art - stunning. It boldly proclaimed who you represented.

This got me thinking. Our Father in heaven wants us to put on the breastplate of righteousness. He wants us to show the world who we stand for. He wants us to shine bright as warriors for Him. And of course, He doesn't want us taken out in battle!

Don't Waste it!

II Corinthians 5:21 - 6:1 says: **"God made him who had no sin to be sin for us, so that in him we might become the righteousness of God. As God's fellow workers we urge you not to receive God's grace in vain."** In other words, God made Jesus pay the price for us to have this breastplate to show the world His righteousness. So, please, don't waste it by not wearing it!

When studying Roman armor, I found out that about two hundred years before Paul wrote Ephesians, the soldiers supplied their own armor. That meant if they were poor they probably couldn't afford a breastplate (or most of the other armor). It was expensive! Many of the soldiers showed up for battle without pieces of armor they needed for protection. This of course meant there were many casualties do to lack of armor. But, by the time of the birth of Christ, the Roman Empire required their soldiers to have a full set of armor. The soldiers, though, had to pay for it. The money they normally would have received at the start of their service went to paying for their armor.

Okay, what does that have to do with us? Well, our armor was paid for by Jesus, our Lord, on the cross. That is why Paul is saying, **"Don't receive the grace of God in vain."** Again, don't waste it! It cost a lot! In fact, it's the priciest outfit out there! Also, just like the Roman government we are also commanded to put on the **"full armor of God."** With this in mind, let's get an understanding of **"righteousness"** and what putting on this **"breastplate"** looks like.

Righteousness

"Righteousness" is translated from the Greek work *dikaiosunee*. Its basic definition is doing or being what is just and right. At this point you might be thinking: "I'm not always just or right!" Actually, as we read previously only one man was, Jesus Christ. Romans 4:25 tells us that **"He was delivered over to death for our sins and was raised to life for our justification." "Justification"** [*dikaios*] is from the same root word that **"righteousness"** is translated from. It was a judicial decision to establish a man right by an acquittal from guilt. A simple way to say this is: "It's just as if you didn't sin." Your slate is wiped clean! No record of wrongdoing! All I can say is... Hallelujah! We are all free to start over, learn from our mistakes and do what's right.

If you're wondering: "but, I keep making mistakes, committing sins." Guess what? That's good you figured that out! 1 John 1:8, 9 says **"If we claim to be without sin, we deceive ourselves and the truth is not in us. If we confess our sins, he is faithful and just and will forgive us ours sins and purify us from all unrighteousness."**

Then 1 John 2:1,2 says, **"...we have one who speaks to the Father in our defense - Jesus Christ, the Righteous One. He is the atoning sacrifice for our sins, and not only for ours but also for the sins of the whole world."**

I hope you are getting this. Yes, we will sin sometimes. This is not a license to sin clause. It's the ultimate expression of God's love that we can continually be forgiven and start over. If you see yourself the way God sees you - forgiven, justified, righteous... then you will shine bright and reflect His glory. Not only will you shine but you will also be protected from the onslaught of Satan's lies, one of them being condemnation.

⁓

Condemned!

I use to live in the Bronx and very often I would pass by apartments in the South Bronx that were condemned. The windows were boarded up but something was done to make it look a little nicer to those of us traveling on the Cross Bronx Expressway. The wood in the windows was painted to make it look like people were living in the buildings. I remember painted flower boxes, curtains and even painted people looking out the windows. It was an interesting way to make a dangerous, rat and cockroach infested building look nice!

Well, sometimes we do the same thing. We try to look all nice on the outside but inwardly out thoughts are how horrible we are. We don't take seriously the truth that Jesus paid the price for our sins. The idea here is that we can take the condemned sign down, the boards off the windows and let the light shine in. It's time to exterminate those creepy thoughts of how messed up we are.

Romans 6:6 says, **"For we know that our old self was cruci-fied with him so that the body of sin might be done away with, that we should no longer be slaves to sin"**. Instead of being a slave to sin (which so many people in the world are without even knowing) we can do what verse 11 says: **"...count yourselves dead to sin but alive to God in Christ Jesus."**

When we do this Romans 8:1, 2 lives for us. **"Therefore, there is now no condemnation for those who are in Christ Jesus, be-cause through Christ Jesus the law of the Spirit of life set me**

free from the law of sin and death." No condemnation means you can get off your case and focus on walking with Jesus.

There is no reason to close up shop and hang up a condemned sign over our hearts. Forgiveness is always available. God wants to forgive you and clean you up. There's another thing God wants, which of course the devil doesn't want, and that is for us also to forgive.

⌒

Forgive... No Way... Yes, Way!

Actually that's Satan's **way** of handling people who have sinned against us. II Corinthians 2:10, 11 **"...if there was anything to forgive - I have forgiven in the sight of Christ for your sake, in order that Satan might not outwit us. For we are not unaware of his schemes."**

When we stay in bitterness by refusing to forgive we are being outsmarted, plain and simple. Bitter, unforgiving hearts make for miserable people and well... the devil just stole the joy that Jesus came to bring.

Ephesians 4:31 is also plain and maybe not simple but very clear. **"...forgive as the Lord forgave you."** If you are thinking that what someone did was just too hurtful and you would never do something so bad then you'll need to think of what Jesus said from the cross as He was dying. **"Father, forgive them, for they do not know what they are doing."** (Luke 23:34) Jesus saw the people for who they were, people who were influenced by Satan without knowledge of the truth.

Satan manipulates people to do his stealing, killing and destroying. We are to follow Christ's example and forgive and

41

recognize that the people who hurt us through their sinful behavior are really clueless to how they are being used. They are like puppets on strings. He manipulates them by "pulling strings" like greed, pride, envy, lust, anger… to do his evil work. If we refuse to forgive then we are giving him another string to pull.

So if you do not want to be manipulated or outsmarted by Satan follow Jesus' way of dealing with sinners (including yourself), forgive. This frees you up to be who God called you to be – an instrument of righteousness – God's righteousness not self-righteousness.

Self-righteousness

At this point it's important to recognize that this righteousness is not from what we do. We don't earn it. Paul states in Philippians 3:8-9 that he wanted to be found in Christ **"not having a righteousness of my own that comes from the law, but that which is through faith in Christ - the righteousness that comes from God and is by faith."** Basically it's reminding ourselves that by God's grace through Christ we do right things. It's not by our own ability but by God working in us. **"For it is God who works in you to will and to act according to his good purpose."** (Philippians 2:13) This is how we can be His instruments of righteousness!

Instruments of Righteousness

"…Offer yourselves to God, as those who have been brought from death to life; … as instruments of righteousness." (Romans 6:13) If we switch our focus from condemning ourselves and others or self-righteously noting how right we do things, we can then focus on who God made us to be in Christ. Ephesians 2:8-10 explains it so clearly. **"For it is by grace you have been saved, through faith - and not of yourselves, it is a gift of God - not by works, so that no one can boast. For we are God's workmanship, created in Christ Jesus to do good works, which God prepared in advance for us to do."**

We are **"God's workmanship;"** His **"Instruments of righteousness."** That means we all have work to do. **"Good works!"** When we put on our **"breastplate of righteousness"** we are ready mentally to do those "**good works which God prepared in advance for us to do.**"

Solid Protection for Our Hearts

Satan's major attack is at the heart of who we are. Proverbs 4:23 tells us: **"Above all else, guard your heart for it is the wellspring of life."** If he can get us to take off our breastplate or never put it on then we are open targets for his lies. He will either convince us that we can never do things right or fill us with pride. He'd like us to be either bent over in shame and condemnation, or boasting and judgmental. Both are harmful. Not just to us though, but also to those around us. It is so important for us to protect our hearts so that we can truly live out God's calling. That is why He's given us a breastplate. It's to protect our hearts from believing lies and instead believe who we are in Christ. Righteous!

How Do We Put on this Breastplate?

Putting on the "**breastplate of righteousness**" is simply reminding yourself (forcefully if need be) that you are a "**new creation**

in Christ." (II Corinthians 5:17) That Jesus paid the price by His death for us to be free from sins enslavement. That you now are "**God's workmanship;**" His "**instrument of righteousness.**" Step out each day <u>expecting</u> to do the good works God prepared for you to do.

When you see yourself the way God sees you, forgiven, justified, righteous... loved, then you will reign in life, shining bright with your heart fully protected because you are wearing "**the breastplate of righteousness.**"

Eight

The Footwear of Peace

Ready with the Secure Footwear of Peace
"Stand firm... with your feet fitted with the readiness
that comes from the gospel of peace," Ephesians 6:15

Our **"feet fitted"** already gives you an idea that this foot attire is not like a flimsy flip flop, spiked heels or a loafer. This was footwear that you couldn't just slip off or even slip with. Once you put it on, it enabled you to: stand firm, walk miles and run full force. In fact, it was made with durable leather straps that were attached to a thick sole which had spikes for traction. Also, they really hurt if you kicked someone! The straps would be tied firmly around the ankle and calf. In the winter, soldiers would wrap their feet with wool and then fit their feet in this sandal like footwear.

Think for a moment. What does a good pair of sneakers or work boots mean to you? Now, think of what it feels like to be barefoot on a cold or hot, rocky surface. Let's go a step further. Think of how you would feel if you were barefoot at a construction site with nails, broken glass, wood splinters, chewing tobacco...!

Are you getting the significance of why we need good footwear, spiritually? We need to be able to take firm stances as well as run with perseverance. We also need to walk through some very dangerous terrain without falling. Thankfully God has given us great footwear, which comes with a very important and beneficial characteristic, **"readiness."**

Are You Ready?

The Greek word **"readiness"** is *hetoimusia.* In the King James Version, it is translated **"preparation."** If the preparation is done then that means you are ready. What does that look like in your everyday life? Whether it's getting dinner on the table, passing a test or doing a presentation at work, there are preparations that need to transpire before hand. Then, there's that point in time when you are ready. You can now say "dinner is served" or "bring it on!"

When we understand and prepare our minds with the gospel of peace, we too are ready. Ready for whatever comes our way! We too can say, "Bring it on!" What a great mental state to be in - prepared with the gospel of peace.

Peace, Please!

Most people are yearning for this peace. That was my greatest desire before I came to know Christ. My life was such a mess. There was "drama" everywhere. All I wanted was a stress free day! Anxiety, suspicion, anger and shame were constantly pulling me in different directions. I remember hearing about a class on the Bible. The promo for the class had a list of benefits that the Bible offered. One was peace. That was all I needed to sign up. Peace, please!

Peace, To Join Together

I always thought peace was just about feeling calm and tranquil. Which you will, but it really goes much deeper than that. Peace, *eirene* in Greek comes from the root word *eiro*, which means to join together. That definition made me think... What does to join together have to do with peace? Ephesians 2:12-14 came to mind.

"Remember that at that time you were separate from Christ, excluded from citizenship in Israel and foreigners to the covenants of the promise, without hope and without God in the world. But now in Christ Jesus you who once were far away have been brought near through the blood of Christ. For he himself is our peace, who has made the two one and has destroyed the barrier, the dividing wall of hostility,"

This section of scripture plainly shows us the ultimate joining together, taking two and making it one!

Then verses 17and 18 goes further to explain this gospel of peace.
"He came and preached peace to you who were far away and to those who were near. For through him we both have access to the Father by one Spirit."

When you step back and look at this section of scripture you'll realize this **"peace"** has many layers. Peace on earth amongst all

47

people. Peace with each other in the body of Christ. Peace with God in Christ. Peace in our hearts.

⌣⟶

Peace on Earth

"I urge, then, first of all, that requests, prayers, intercession and thanksgiving be made for everyone - for kings and all those in authority, that we may live peaceful and quiet lives in all godliness and holiness. This is good, and pleases God our Savior, who wants all men to be saved and to come to a knowledge of the truth." I Timothy 2:1-4

At the birth of Jesus Christ, the angels proclaimed **"Glory to God in the highest and on earth peace to men on whom His favor rests."** Luke 2:14.

God's desire for all mankind is that we all would be saved and know the truth. Just think of what it would look like if that happened. No more wars! Every human being living peaceful and quiet lives, at one with each other. That's God's heart and He is pleased when nations are living at peace with each other. But, then again, we are in a battle and our opposing force, Satan, continually leads people away from the truth. This causes turmoil, divisions… wars.

Thankfully we have the hope of a new heaven and earth to look forward to. When all who are saved will live in peace together for all eternity! Until then, though we are to pray for people's salvation. The more people who truly follow Jesus and let His peace rule in their hearts, the more peace on earth!

Peace within the Church

Romans 14:19 is pretty direct. **"Let us therefore make every effort to do what leads to peace and mutual edification."** The believers in Rome were obviously getting on each other cases over what they ate. Verse 20 says: **"Do not destroy the work of God for the sake of food."** This might not be the case in many churches today, but there are other issues that cause divisions amongst Christians. Verse 1 tells us **"Accept him whose faith is weak, without passing judgment on disputable matters."** How many disputable matters are we passing judgments on? Ephesians 4:2-3 tells us to **"be completely humble and gentle; be patient, bearing with one another in love. Make every effort to keep the unity of the Spirit in the bond of peace."** Notice it's the **"bond of peace."**

It's so important for us to get this. We as the body of Christ, the church, should be at one with each other, at peace, bond together! Colossians 3:15 couldn't get any clearer! **"Let the peace of Christ rule in your hearts, since as members of one body you were called to peace."** Notice it says: **"rule."** To rule means to call the shots. It also says we **"were called to peace."** The idea here is to not to be divisive, judgmental, envious, selfish... James 3:16-18 says: **"For where you have envy and selfish ambition, there you find disorder and every evil practice. But wisdom that comes from heaven is first of all pure; then peace loving, considerate, submissive, full of mercy and good fruit, impartial and sincere. Peacemakers who sow peace raise a harvest of righteousness."**

Seriously, this **"gospel of peace"** is armor we have to wear continually! The body of Christ needs to stand unified, one with each other. We all need to be **"peacemakers"** and **"sow peace"** so that we **"raise a harvest of righteousness."** That's something that our adversary does not want to see - **"a harvest of righteousness"** which, basically, is more territory won over for Christ our Lord!

Peace with God in Christ

James 4:1 tells us the reason for so much of the division in the church. **"What causes fights and quarrels among you? Don't they come from the desires that battle within you?"** What are the desires that battle within us? Verse 6 reveals the one factor that causes most of our inner battles: **"God opposes the proud but gives grace to the humble."**

Pride, another way God describes it is in verse 4: **"friendship with the world."** Being a friend of the world is looking for recognition through man's standards. Who and what does the world highly esteem? Just look at a magazine rack! Physical beauty, money, educational degrees, talent, muscles, sex… None of these things are wrong in themselves. Actually, God our Creator gives us all our abilities. But when we become all about how much money we make, or what universities we went to, or how much good works we did… this always leads to pride. When we live our lives for the recognition we receive through them we forfeit our peace with God.

Romans 12:2 tells us: **"Do not conform to the pattern of this world, but be transformed by the renewing of you mind. Then you will be able to test and approve what God's will is - his good, pleasing and perfect will."** Then verse 3 says: **"…Do not think of yourself more highly than you ought."** Verse 5 tells us why. **"So in Christ we who are many form one body, and each member belongs to all the others."**

The world would have us all be about our rights and privileges. God is saying: "humble yourself, come to me as a child and I'll take care of you. I'll lift you up." (See James 4:10) Another word for humble is submit. When we submit we agree to follow someone's directions. To have peace with God, to be at one with Him we need to submit to Him. James 4:7 **"Submit yourselves, then, to God. Resist the devil, and he will flee from you. Come near to God and He will come near to you."** Close to God, together with Him, about His business, about His will, about His heart... That's peace with God in Christic!

Peace in Our Hearts

It's pretty easy to see how the root word *eiro*, to join, fits into understanding peace in the previous scenarios. But, how does that play out in our own minds and hearts? The calm and tranquil state we actually feel. Well, there are two women who can help us understand this: Martha and Mary.

"As Jesus and his disciple were on their way, he came to a village where a woman named Martha opened her home to him. She had a sister called Mary, who sat at the Lord's feet listening to what he said. But Martha was distracted by all the preparations that had to be made. She came to him ad asked, "Lord, don't you care that my sister has left me to do the work by myself? Tell her to help me!"

"Martha, Martha," the Lord answered, "you are worried and upset about many things, but only one thing is needed. Mary has chosen what is better, and it will not be taken away from her." Luke 10:38-42

The Greek word for **"worried"** is *merimnao,* which means divided into many parts. It comes from the word *meris,* which means "one part" and is translated **"one thing"** which is what Mary chose. **"The preparations that had to be made"** is translated from one word: *diakonia,* which means service. According to Jesus they didn't have to be made **"only one thing"** was needed... obviously it was to sit and listen to Jesus at that moment.

Martha was **"worried and upset over many things."** **"Upset"** is *turbazomai* which one could almost guess what that means in English: turbo charged, in a frenzy! Most of us women and some of you men get this. You have a bunch of people over and you feel compelled to have everything go just right. You race around to make sure everyone is comfortable, that the food is cooking properly, that the house is clean... Then you notice someone who should be helping out and they're sitting with the guest, enjoying themselves! There's one more thing to agitate you. I find it amusing that Martha was so annoyed that she interrupted Jesus to complain... and not just about her sister but about Him not caring!

Notice, Mary chose what was better, and Jesus was not going to allow it to be taken away from her. He wasn't going to give in to Martha's tirade. We also can choose not to get in a frenzy and to worry but instead to listen to Jesus and He will take our side too! In John 14:27 Jesus tells us: **"Peace I leave with you; my peace I give you. I do not give to you as the world gives. Do not let your hearts be troubled and do not be afraid."**

We can choose not to be in a rush all the time. We can decide to slow down and not give up our peace. So often, like Martha, we have too many things we are trying to get done that are consuming our thoughts. We need to decide what is really important and also to give ourselves enough time to do it. Like Mary we can choose to listen to Jesus who does speak to our hearts as well as the fact that we have God's Word to go to for guidance in any situation we are in.

Remember this is **"Armor."** Without peace we are easy targets, tripping and falling over every obstacle. In this battle we need to be marching forward, ready and secure in the peace of God in Christ so...

"Do not be anxious [*merimnao*] about anything, but in everything, by prayer and petition, with thanksgiving present your requests to God. And the peace of God, which transcends all understanding will guard your hearts and your minds in Christ Jesus." Philippians 4:6-7

This is your choice. In every situation, with every person, in every moment to be at one with God in Christ, peaceful!

Nine

The Shield of Faith

"In addition to all this, take up the shield of faith, with which you can extinguish all the flaming arrows of the evil one."
Ephesians 6:16

This verse starts with **"in addition."** Along with the belt of truth, breastplate of righteousness and footwear of peace, we have been given other armor that must be worn.

This next piece is HUGE! Huge in what it does for us and in fact... HUGE! The shield, *thureos,* in Greek, was the size of a door. The root word for shield is actually the word door - *thura.* It was covered in layers of leather and then soaked in water. This enabled it to extinguish flaming arrows. A soldier would stand behind it for full protection.

Notice it's for full protection. **"...you can extinguish <u>all</u> the flaming arrows of the evil one."** We don't have to get burnt... ever. We have a fire extinguisher! It's the one thing needed to escape hell, as well as the destructive forces of evil. Most Christians just need to know how to use it.

Before we study how to use our shield we need to be aware of what those **"flaming arrows"** look like in our everyday lives. In chapter three I touched on some of the **"devil's schemes." "Flaming arrows"** are definitely his way of scheming to take us out of the battle! I think it's worth taking a further look at some of what he uses. We, like any soldier, will put up our shield for protection when we see one of these **"flaming arrows"** heading toward us.

Flaming Arrows

Temptations to sin are definitely highly effective arrows. James 1:14-15 tells us that temptations drag us away to sin which leads to death. Sin, plain and simple is disobeying God. When we sin in any form we will experience the opposite of true life. Sin usually feels okay, if not good for the moment but it always has consequences we wished we never had to deal with. Consequences such as addictions, broken relationships, financial problems, job losses, jail time... and the list goes on!

Another way the evil one tries to take us out is troubles. Whether its persecution, insults, hardships, difficulties... anything that causes us to feel weak he will use to urge us to give up or give in to sin. In II Corinthians 12:7-10, a messenger from Satan was sent to Paul to torment him. Paul prayed to have this messenger taken away. Jesus had a better solution and told him **"My grace is sufficient for you, for my power is made perfect in weakness."** Verse 10 Paul states that he delighted **"in weaknesses, in insults, in hardships, in persecutions, in difficulties. For when I am weak, then I am strong."**

All of us experience difficulties or trials. That's what battlefields are made of. Rather than let weaknesses, insults, hardships, persecutions or any trying situation cause us to give up or give in to sin we can recognize them for what they are, **"flaming arrows."** More important we have to see them as opportunities to use our faith and see Christ's power in us at work. Again this is HUGE! It's what sets us apart from all humanity, our faith in our risen Lord and Savior, Jesus Christ!

So think for a moment. What are your difficulties right now? Are you dealing with a difficult person at work or at home? Are you being ridiculed for your faith or even persecuted? Are you feeling weak due to an illness either you have or someone close to you? Or are you being tempted to do things you know aren't right? A flaming arrow is any circumstance in which the objection is to get us to stop living for God in light of eternity. Some people like Stephen (Acts 7) and others who were listed among those who were commended for their faith in Hebrews 11, died physical deaths due to persecution but never gave up their faith. They will be rewarded for their stands and their lives are still bearing testimonies for us today. Basically, to be taken out by a flaming arrow is put aside your faith and to accept a lie that Satan has given you.

In 1 Peter 5:8, 9 we are told to **"be self-controlled and alert. Your enemy the devil prowls around like a roaring lion looking for someone to devour. Resist him standing firm in the faith."** It's important for us to recognize his tactics. To be **"alert"** to them so we can stand **"firm in the faith."** So I urge you to take the time now to note what he is using to try to take you out. Once you recognize them the next step is to… step behind your **"shield of faith!"**

Standing Behind Our Shield

Hebrews, chapter 11, is a great place to go and see what standing behind your faith looks like.

Now, faith is being sure of what we hope for and certain of what we do not see. This is what the ancients were commended for."
Hebrews 11:1, 2

The rest of Hebrews 11 describes what faith looks like. It is a record of men and women who knew verse 6 to be true. **"And without faith it is impossible to please God, because anyone who comes to him must believe that he exists and that he rewards those who earnestly seek him."**

I recommend that you read Hebrews 11 and take time to picture what it looked like for these people to live out their faith.

For example: What was it like for Noah to build an ark? By the way, he didn't have a lumber store to go to! Think about how many years it took, possibly over 100! Think of what his evil neighbors were saying. Is there anything you are doing in obedience to God that seems to be taking a long time without bearing much or any fruit? Like Noah, hang in there so you also can experience the rewards of your faith.

What about Abraham and Sarah? A hundred year old man and a ninety-year-old woman still waiting for the baby they were told they would have. They knew it would have to be a miracle. Are you in need of a miracle or still waiting for a promise of God to come to pass? Think of the moment Sarah first felt the baby move in her! Think of what a ninety-year-old pregnant woman looks like! Think of the testimony this was to them and those around them. Now imagine what it will be like when your need is met. (We are told in Ephesians 3:20 to ask and imagine!) It will be another testimony of God's great faithfulness to share with others.

When reading Hebrews 11 we see many different examples of faith. There's Moses, who **"by faith when he had grown up,**

58

refused to be known as the son of the Pharaoh's daughter. He chose to be mistreated along with the people of God rather than to enjoy the pleasures of sin for a short time." Very often, faith is described by getting a prayer answered but it's so much bigger than that. It's deciding to follow God's directions even if that means leaving the lap of luxury to live for God. Sometimes that means you will be mistreated, ridiculed and in some places persecuted by others. Are you willing to obey God even if it means you might be ridiculed or persecuted by others? Maybe even lose your job?

Then there's Rahab, the prostitute, who by faith welcomed the men who came to spy out the promise land. She actually hid them on a rooftop under stalks of flax. (Read Joshua 2 for the full story.) Take a moment to picture that. First of all, her resume was a bit shoddy... a prostitute! What she did have was... guts! That fierceness came from knowing that the God of the Israelites was extremely powerful and she wanted to make sure her and her family lived through the invasion. Also, the word she spoke to them **"I know the Lord has given this land to you... all who live in this country are melting in fear because of you."** (Joshua 2:9) encouraged the spies who reported this message to Joshua. What about you? What can you do now that will help others know Christ? None of us are perfect. We all sin but God can still use us to bring deliverance to others lives. By the way, if you look up the Christ line in the book of Matthew you'll find that Rahab is listed!

These are just a few examples from Hebrews 11. I do suggest that you spend some time looking up the accounts of these people and picturing what it looked like for them. Hebrews 12:1 says **"Therefore, since we are surrounded by such a great cloud of witnesses, let us throw off everything that hinders us and the sin that so easily entangles, and let us run with perseverance the race marked out for us."** These witnesses are meant to be inspiring examples for us! What inspiration can you take from their lives? How can their testimonies help you run the race marked out for you?

$$\smile\longrightarrow$$

The Focus of Our Faith, Jesus Christ!

Then, in verse 2 we see the greatest example of all and the focal point of our faith! **"Let us fix our eyes on Jesus, the author and perfecter of our faith, who for the joy set before him endured the cross, scorning its shame, and sat down at the right hand of the throne of God."** Our faith is based on Jesus and what He did on the cross for us! We can stand behind the fact that He died and rose from the dead as complete payment for our sins and our salvation!

He is our Lord and Savior and He understands what we are going through <u>today</u>, and wants to help us. **"Therefore, since we have a great high priest who has gone through the heavens, Jesus the Son of God, let us hold firmly to the faith we profess. For we do not have a high priest who is unable to sympathize with our weaknesses, but we have one who has been tempted in every way, just as we are yet was without sin. Let us then approach the throne of grace with confidence, so that we may receive mercy and find grace to help in our time of need."** Hebrews 4:14-16

So remember, when a **"flaming arrow"** comes your way, you have a shield! A HUGE shield! It is **"the faith we profess"** – faith to ask Jesus for help knowing He's there for us! Faith to obey God knowing **"He rewards those who earnestly seek Him."**

"**This is the victory that has overcome the world, even our faith. Who is it that overcomes the world? Only he who believes that Jesus is the Son of God.**" 1 John 5:4. Do you believe? Then you too have faith that overcomes the world and... have been given "**the helmet of salvation!**"

Ten

The Helmet of Salvation

"Take the helmet of salvation..." Ephesians 6:17

The helmet that the Roman soldiers wore was like the breast-plate in that it served two purposes. It protected another very vital organ, the brain! It also was adorned with beautiful engravings. These helmets were works of art. Like the breastplate, if you were wearing this piece of armor, you stood out in the crowd.

For us, the significance is that once we put this **"helmet"** on we will be thinking as one who is saved and has a new life in Christ. This mindset, you will see, is for our protection as well as attracting others to Christ. We all want this! That is why it's important to understand the significance of our salvation and why it's a helmet for us, and then, of course, to wear it.

Salvation

"Salvation," ***soteerion*** in Greek, means to be brought into a safe place; no longer in bondage and subject to destruction. So simple, but do we get it? Have we saturated our minds with the significance of what it means to no longer be in bondage, no longer subject to destruction? This is not just a promise for the future. Indeed, the hope of eternity in a perfect world is the major factor of our salvation and we will cover how the hope is a major part of our mindset but, it's critical for us to realize that we are saved… today!

Saved Today!

"…Now is the time of God's favor, now is the day of salvation."
II Corinthians 6:2

Our salvation started the day we accepted Christ as Lord. Romans 10:9-12 states very plainly how to be saved. **"That if you confess with your mouth, "Jesus is Lord" and believe in your heart that God raised him from the dead, you will be saved. For it is with your heart that you believe and are justified, and it is with your mouth that you confess and are saved. As the Scripture says,** (quoted from Isaiah 28:16) **"Anyone who trusts in him will never be put to shame." For there is no difference between Jew and Gentile - the same Lord is Lord of all and richly blesses all who call on him."** Then verse 13 quotes from Joel 2:32 **"Everyone who calls on the name of the Lord will be saved."** At that point we get to live in God's favor, richly blessed… saved. We are no longer under the control of the evil forces that are wrecking havoc in the world, but it's up to us to live, aware of the freedom we now have.

For he has rescued us from the dominion of darkness and brought us into the kingdom of the Son he loves, in whom we have redemption, the forgiveness of sins.
Colossians 1:13, 14

We have been rescued from the dominion of darkness! Satan does not want us to truly believe this because when we do we are no longer subject to his domineering ways. He really has no power over us. We literally allow him to mess with our lives by not accepting the full benefit package of a saved son or daughter of God. Part of our salvation is that we no longer have to be pushed around by evil forces, slaves to sin. If we do allow ourselves to get tricked and we sin, forgiveness is always available.

When we allow the truth of what we have to soak in, we will experience the freedom we have in Christ. This is part of what **"take up the helmet of salvation"** looks like. It's deciding to live as free men and women for God in Christ. Free from the debilitating effects of sin because we choose to obey God through the power He has given us in Christ. It's not about how good we are but how gracious God is to rescue us and give us this armor!

It's a choice, which requires a thought process. Brainpower! Do you understand now, why it's a helmet? When we put on the **"helmet of salvation"** we are reminding ourselves that we are saved from any reason to sin. We no longer have to live in: jealousy, hatred, judgmental attitudes, anxiety, lust, condemnation ... We can put those corrupt thoughts off and put on our new, saved, Christ-like minds.

Each of us needs to look at what we've been given when we accepted Christ Jesus as Lord. We also need to remind ourselves what life was like before our salvation, or for some of us, when we lived apart from Christ. We can't get nonchalant, too casual, about what we've been saved from. Think for a moment what it must be like to be rescued out of a burning building or pulled out of a mineshaft after days in darkness and rubble. Think of the relief you would feel! Now think of what you have been saved from – **"the dominion of darkness"** and hell! But, unlike those saved from a physical disaster that go back to the same life they lived before, you are saved to live a new life in **"the kingdom of the Son He loves."** Spend time rejoicing in what you've been saved from and what you have been saved to. Saved from the dominating forces of darkness to Christ's kingdom where Christ reigns!

Living in Light of Eternity

Another aspect of wearing your **"helmet of salvation"** is to live in light of eternity. We have the hope of eternal life in pure perfection to encourage us when we need it, which is often. II Corinthians 4:16-18 states it clearly: **"Therefore we do not lose heart. Though outwardly we are wasting away, yet inwardly, we are being renewed day by day. For our light and momentary troubles are achieving for us an eternal glory that far outweighs them all. So we fix our eyes not on what is seen, but on what is unseen. For what is seen is temporary, but what is unseen is eternal."** Fix our eyes on the goal: **"...clothed with our heavenly dwelling, so that what is mortal may be swallowed up by life. Now it is God who has made us for this very purpose and has given us the Spirit as a deposit, guaranteeing what is to come."** II Corinthians 5:4-5

There is so much to look forward to. **"...we are looking forward to a new heaven and a new earth, the home of righteousness."** II Peter 3:13 Spend time thinking what it's going to be like to see Jesus face to face, to see your loved ones again, to understand all things, to hang out with lions, tigers and bears...

unafraid. How nice it will be to not have to struggle with sin and to never grieve again.

Just think what it's going to be like when the trumpet blows! **For the Lord himself will come down from heaven, with a loud command, with the voice of the archangel and with the trumpet call of God, and the dead in Christ will rise first. After that, we who are still alive and are left will be caught up together with them in the clouds, to meet the Lord in the air. And so we will be with the Lord forever. Therefore encourage each other with these words."** I Thessalonians 4:16-18. Notice it says, **"encourage each other with these words".** Spend time thinking about what that's going to be like. It will encourage you!

Then I Thessalonians 5:8-11 tells us how we should live in light of the hope: **"...let us be self-controlled, putting on faith and love as a breastplate and the hope of salvation as a helmet. For God did not appoint us to suffer wrath but to receive salvation through our Lord Jesus Christ. He died for us so that whether we are awake or asleep, we may live together with him. Therefore, encourage one another and build each other up..."** Notice it says **"be self-controlled..."** The knowledge of the hope is to also help us live for Christ now. Knowing that one day we will meet the Lord in the air helps us get through today! Also, knowing what we do today, can have an effect on all eternity is also part of wearing **"the helmet of salvation".**

Step Back and Look at the Big Picture

I'm an artist. I paint murals on tile. There is one art technique that I use regularly. It's stepping back and looking at the big picture. Very often while painting my perspective can be off and the details that I'm adding are messing up the artwork. This is great advice for life too. Are you living life with eternity in mind? Are the details of your life enhancing the big picture or making a mess?

Now in case this is a little too artsy for you a builder's perspective is given in I Corinthians 3:11-15 **"For no one can lay any foundation other than the one already laid, which is Jesus Christ. If any man builds on this foundation using gold, silver, costly stones, wood, hay or straw his work will be shown for what it is, because the Day will bring it to light. It will be revealed with fire, and the fire will test the quality of each man's work. If what he has built survives, he will receive his reward. If it is burned up, he will suffer loss; he himself will be saved, but only as one escaping through the flames."**

Do you realize that what you do here has an effect in all eternity? Your life can draw others to Christ or push people away. You could be building with gold or hay? Or... not lifting a finger, having no effect at all! You see through our lives others can know Christ. That's what building with gold and silver looks like. Ephesians 4:12 tells us that those with gift ministries are **"to prepare God's people for works of service, so that, the body of Christ may be built up until we all reach unity in the faith and in the knowledge of the Son of God."** Our mission on earth is to help each other have a strong relationship with Jesus. This mission affects those we help receive salvation and grow as well as our own eternity. We will be rewarded for our works of service that in some way helped others know Jesus.

⌣⟶

Rewards

Now I know, for me, I am usually not thinking about rewards when I am in the process of doing works of service. Philippians 2:13 says, **"for it is God who works in you to will and to act according**

to His good purpose." Often, good works flow through us via God's inspiration. Many times I find myself thanking God for leading me into a situation where I got to be a blessing. It would be nice if it was always that way, but it's not.

There are those times when we know we should help but it's inconvenient. Or the time we should confront someone who is causing harm to themselves or others but we know it's going to make them upset. There are the times it's easier to lie or keep something that doesn't belong to us when we know who it might belong to... The list goes on. This is when knowing II Corinthians 5:10 will come in handy. **"For we all must appear before the judgment seat of Christ, that each one may receive what is due him for the things done while in the body, whether good or bad."**

This is not to be taken lightly. Rewards are spoken of all throughout God's Word. He wants us to be aware of the rewards we will get for doing the works of service He has called us to. In Matthew 16:26-27, Jesus gives us a clear picture of this: **"What good will it be for a man if he gains the whole world yet forfeits his soul? ...For the Son of Man is going to come in his Father's glory with his angels, and then he will reward each person according to what he has done."** Making right decisions based on knowing we will get rewarded for doing the right thing is another aspect of wearing our **"helmet of salvation."** Our Father is aware that sometimes we need incentive, just like any child!

⌐⌐⌐

Be Attractive

Remember this **"helmet of salvation"** is also attractive. Just like the roman soldier's helmet was. When he wore his helmet he stood out in a crowd.

When your thought life is about knowing you are loved as a child of God, saved from the forces of evil and on your way to your home of righteousness, you can't help but rejoice. People with smiling faces and sparkling eyes are way more attractive than frowning or angry faces. Also, people who are eternity minded aren't about themselves but know that they are here for a far greater purpose.

"For we are God's workmanship, created in Christ Jesus to do good works, which God prepared in advance for us to do."
Ephesians 2:10

We are God's works of art with a functional purpose, to do the good works He's given each of us to do. Live your life living out your purpose and you will be... looking good!

Eleven

The Sword of the Spirit

"...and the sword of the Spirit which is the word of God."
Ephesians 6:17

As you have probably noticed, each piece of armor has different benefits. Primarily they are for protection but also for preparedness, stability and attraction. The next piece of armor is specifically for offence.

A sword, now that's dangerous! Dangerous for our opponent! This particular sword [*makaira*] was known for its razor sharpness on both sides. It was what Peter used to slice a man's ear off! (John 18:10)

Think of what you would do if someone were coming at you with a razor sharp sword? I'd imagine you'd take off running or possibly... faint! The evil forces, which we battle against, are aware of the sharpness of this sword. Remember it is the **"sword of the Spirit."** Another way of saying this is, it is the sword of God. It doesn't get fiercer than that! A sword given to us by God! Our spiritual enemies know we can wreak havoc against their evil plans with this dangerous weapon. II Corinthians

10:4-5 describes our weapons very clearly. **"The weapons we fight with... have divine power to demolish strong holds. We demolish arguments and ever pretension that sets itself up against the knowledge of God, and we take captive every though to make it obedient to Christ."** That is why Satan's major plan is to keep the world from hearing God's Word. Satan's next step is to cause people to doubt it.

⸺

Every Word that God Speaks

"It is written: Man does not live on bread alone, but on every word that comes from the mouth of God."
Matthew 4:4

The Greek word in both Ephesians 6:17 and Matthew 4:4 translated "**word**" is *rhema*, which means: that which is spoken. Right before Jesus was led into the wilderness He had been baptized and God spoke aloud **"This is my Son, whom I love; with him I am well pleased."** Matthew 3:17

The first two of the three temptations, recorded in Matthew 4:1-11, start with **"If you are the Son of God..."** It's obvious that the devil was trying to manipulate Jesus to obey him by using the small but typically effective word that causes people to doubt: **"if."** He tried to make Jesus feel like He had to prove the word God had spoken. Jesus responded to each temptation with **"It is written..."** He took out His **"sword,"** what God had said, and slashed each temptation with it. In following Jesus' example, never do what Satan tells you to do - even if it doesn't look like sin. Satan told Jesus to turn stones into bread. (Matt.4:3) Jesus could have done that. He later turned water into wine (John 2:9) and used a boys lunch to feed thousands (John 6:11). But to do something that looks good for the wrong motives is definitely a scheme of Satan. It's a good idea to ask: "Why am I doing this, really?" Like Jesus we need to take up our **"sword"** against temptation.

Hebrews 4:12 says, **"For the word of God is living and active. Sharper than any double-edged sword, it penetrates even to dividing soul and spirit, joints and marrow; it judges the thoughts and attitudes of the heart."** It is crucial that we study and know God's Word so that, like Jesus, we also can speak **"It is written..."**

Speak God's Word

Our sword is the spoken word of God. What we read in the bible is God's spoken word recorded by men of God. II Peter 1:20-21 **"Above all else, you must understand that no prophecy of Scripture came about by the prophet's own interpretation. For prophecy never had its origin in the will of man but men spoke from God as they were carried along by the Holy Spirit."**

II Timothy 3:16 and 17 make it clear. **"All scripture is God-breathed and is useful for teaching, rebuking, correcting and training in righteousness so that the man of God may be thoroughly equipped for every good work."** That means the scripture we read came out of God's mouth. He wants us to be thoroughly equipped for every good work we are called to do. Equipped with our sword so we can slash every doubt, fear and temptation that gets in the way of doing the good works God has planned for us. (Ephesians 2:10)

Jesus said it plainly: **"If you remain in me and my words remain in you, ask whatever you wish and it will be given you. This is to my Father's glory, that you bear much fruit, showing yourselves to be my disciples."** (John 15:7, 8) To have Jesus'

"words remain in you" means you remember them so you can speak them to your heart as well as use them to slash any evil influence that would keep you from bearing much fruit.

In case you're thinking "I'm not good at coming up with a scripture verse when I need it quickly." You have help! John 14:26 **"But the Counselor, the Holy Spirit, whom the Father will send in my name, will teach you all things and will remind you of everything I said to you."** If you take the time to study God's word, you can ask Him to remind you of what He has said regarding any situation you are in. Then... speak what He says!

Another simple solution is to take the time and study God's word regarding areas where you are frequently tempted or struggles you are dealing with.

Here are a few examples:

Instead of worrying about something, say:
"I cast this care _____ (fill in the blank) to God because He cares for me. He will take care of this. (I Peter 5:7)

When you are tempted to gossip or say something hurtful, say:
"God wants me to speak only what is helpful for building others up. (Eph. 4:29)

When you feel like you are of no benefit to others, say:
"I am God's workmanship, created in Christ Jesus to do the good works He has prepared for me to do." (Eph.2:10)

If you have a rebellious child, say what Jesus said to Peter:
"I have prayed for you that your faith may not fail and when you do turn back you will strengthen others." (Luke 22:31) Jesus did say "Anyone who has faith in me will do what I have been doing..." (John 14:12)

When you need direction on what to do or where to go, say: "I trust in You, Father, with all my heart. I will not lean on my own understanding but with every step I will ask you for guidance and You will direct my path." (Proverbs 3:5, 6)

If you are struggling financially, say: "God loves a cheerful giver and is able to make all grace abound to me so that I can always have what I need and therefore will abound in every good work." (II Corinthians 9:7, 8)

These are just some examples of what to say to your heart. I encourage you to think through your own areas of struggle and write down what God says regarding them. Then make it a habit to speak these truths to your heart. Like a surgeon you can cut out those cancerous, destructive thoughts with this razor sharp tool.

By speaking the truth to others we can also slash Satan's plans of destruction for them too.

Truth Brings Freedom

"If you hold to my teaching, you are really my disciples. Then you will know the truth, and the truth will set you free." John 8:31, 32

When we speak the truth and people believe it we are slashing their bonds of imprisonment. We are releasing prisoners! We are making known God's **"very great and precious promises so that through them you may participate in the divine nature and escape the corruption in the world caused by evil desires."** (II Peter 1:4) Notice it says **"escape."** Remember, this **"sword"** we have is powerful. It cuts through the snares and entanglements that keep people from truly living free lives. Telling people what they have in Christ is wielding our sword against the enemy.

So, start now! Develop a habit of speaking the truth to yourself and others. When you see, hear or feel any evil influences - pull out your sword. Be an opposing, demolition force against evil. Speak God's Word!

Twelve

Pray!

**"And pray in the Spirit on all occasions
with all kinds of prayers
and requests. With this in mind, be alert and always
keep on praying for all the saints."**
Ephesians 6:18

After reading this verse, I think you get the idea... PRAY! It is not the last thing we do. It is what we do as warriors in God's army! We pray on all occasions as we stay alert and keep on praying!

After looking up the Greek words of this verse one thing really stood out. Prayer is also wielding our sword, the spoken Word of God. In the previous chapter we covered the power of the spoken Word against temptation as well as attacks. Jesus spoke **"It is written"** directly to Satan. In this chapter we will see how we also wield our sword through prayer.

The very first word in this verse in Greek is *dia*. Although it's translated **"and"** it means "by" or "through." There were no verse separations when this was written. The very next words in the Greek text are **"all prayers [***prosuke***] and requests [***deesis***].** This could be translated "take the sword of the spirit which is the spoken Word of God through your prayers and requests praying in every season in the spirit." Basically, use God's Word as the premise for your prayer life.

Before we go any further, I want to say this is not complicated. In fact, the definition for the word **"prayers"** is words spoken to God. The definition for **"requests"** is to ask for something that is needed. Pretty simple!

Talk to Your Father

When Jesus taught his disciples how to pray in Matthew 6:9-15, He started with **"Our Father."** He's your Father, and you are talking to Him. It doesn't have to be eloquent or rehearsed. Like most fathers, He loves you and wants to hear from you!

Okay, with this in mind what are some things you would like to tell Him? (Forget about your needs right now.) What about thanking Him for all He continues to do for you or praising Him for all that He is. Jesus' very next words after **"Our Father"** were **"in heaven, hallowed be your name."**

Praise God!

Psalm 100:4 says **"Enter His gates with thanksgiving and His courts with praise."** Now, it's not God who needs our thanksgiving and praise, but us. As we thank God for His many blessings and speak words of praise to Him we are mentally walking through His gates into His presence.

Light dispels darkness. (Ephesians 5:12-13) Whenever we spend time talking to God about who He is, what He has done and will do, it is like a light bulb that got turned on in our heads. Our hearts become full of how great God is and how much He loves us. Romans 1:21 tells us what happens when people don't give God thanks and praise. **"For although they knew God, they neither glorified him as God nor gave thanks to him, but their thinking became futile and their foolish hearts were darkened."** If you don't want your thinking to be futile and your heart foolish and dark, then... Praise and thank God, regularly!

Now back to the battle, if your thoughts are useful and your heart full of light than you will be an imposing force against evil. Praise builds your faith. It instills in your heart the greatness of our loving, heavenly Father who can and wants to help us. Asking our Father for help when others or we need it becomes the only logical thing to do.

God's Will Be Done

Next thing Jesus said when teaching how to pray is **"Your kingdom come, your will be done on earth as it is in heaven."** (Matt. 6:10) It's been spoken so often but, have we really considered what this means?

First of all, the word **"will"** [*thelo* in Greek] means desire. Desires take place in the center of our hearts. It's what we really want. What God desires, what He really wants, is taking place in heaven. Think about it! Every attribute that describes heaven God desires here on earth. One glorious day that will take place completely. (See Revelations 21) That doesn't mean we don't pray for God's will, what He desires, to come to pass... today! Romans 12:2 tells us to be transformed by the renewing of our minds so we can **"test and approve what God's will is - his good, pleasing and perfect will."** God desires that we have good, pleasing and perfect results in our lives but He also has given us free will to choose to renew our minds, replacing wrong thoughts with the truth from His Word as discussed in chapter five. Praying for God's will to come to pass is definitely a renewed mind process! When we choose to obey Him and pray, He then uses our free will choice to perform His will through our prayers. What a great privilege prayer is!

What does God Want?

Of course, to pray for God's will to come to pass means we need to know what He desires (another important reason to study God's Word.) When you know you are asking God for what He wants, you can be confident that He will answer. Part of the devil's schemes is for people to doubt whether it's God's will for their prayers to be answered. You don't want doubt to be part of the equation when praying. Knowing what God wants nullifies any reason to doubt. (See James 1:6-8)

As in the previous chapter, here are some truths that God desires for us. You'll notice it's what you desire too! These are things we can and should pray for. It's what taking our sword, the spoken word of God, in prayer looks like.

Salvation and Knowing the Truth

"I urge, then, first of all, that requests, prayers, intercessions and thanksgiving be made for kings and all those in authority, that we may live peaceful and quiet lives in all godliness and

holiness. This is good and pleases God our Savior, who wants all men to be saved and to come to a knowledge of the truth."
I Timothy 2: 1-3

What does God want? **"... all men to be saved and to come to a knowledge of the truth."** This is the main reason we pray for the leaders in our country: that the message of salvation can be spread freely to all in peace. Is there anyone you want to be saved and know the truth? I know many of our hearts ache for family members or friends who haven't committed their lives to Christ and are believing lies. Well, we can pray confidently for them knowing God also wants them saved and to know the truth. He then can use our prayers in ways we would never think of to bring these people to Christ. Spend some time asking people what brought them to Christ and you'll get some really interesting stories! Usually, you'll also hear about a mom, dad, grandparent, relative... who continued to pray for them when they were off living the wild life. So take this seriously, start fervently praying for those who aren't saved!

Wise Choices

"If any of you lacks wisdom, he should ask God, who gives generously to all without finding fault, and it will be given to him." James 1:5

God wants us to have wisdom and He gives it freely. Are there any decisions you need to make that wisdom is needed? Notice He isn't looking down wondering why you can't figure it out for yourself or how you got in the predicament you're in. He's not a faultfinder but, a loving Father!

Having All We Need to be Cheerful Givers

"Each man should give what he has decided in his heart to give, not reluctantly or under compulsion, for God loves a cheerful giver. And God is able to make all grace abound to you, so that in all things at all times, having all that you need, you will abound in every good work."
II Corinthians 9:7, 8

Okay! Did you notice? **"God loves a cheerful giver."** I can pray for that for… myself! I'd love to always be a cheerful giver too. The next verse tells us how God makes that available: by making **"all grace abound to you…"** Would you like these verses to depict your life? Again, pray for God's will to be done!

Good Health

"And the prayer offered in faith will make a sick person well; the Lord will raise him up. If he has sinned, he will be forgiven. Therefore confess your sins to each other and pray for each other so that you may be healed. The prayer of a righteous man is powerful and effective."
James 5:15, 16

Healing is available. It's up to us to pray and in some cases ask for forgiveness. Our adversary is very successful in getting in the way of this heartfelt desire of God coming to pass in His children's lives. When people are struggling with a sickness, please don't blame God but blame the stealer, the killer and the destroyer! (See John 10:10) God's heart is that we are healed!

Pray!

Powerful and Effective Pray Warriors

Note the last part of this section of scripture! **"The prayer of a righteous man is powerful and effective".** You have been given the **"breastplate of righteousness."** That makes your prayers **"powerful and effective."** God wants us to take this seriously! We get the privilege to pray prayers that are **"powerful and effective."** Another way to say this is forceful and successful! That means our prayers have extreme results in this battle we are in.

"Pray in the Spirit"

Ephesians 6:18 also says to **"pray in the Spirit."** That's the new you - the spiritual you. The you that relies on the gift of Holy Spirit to direct and fuel your prayer life. II Timothy 1:7 says **"For God did not give us the spirit of timidity, but a spirit of power, of love and of self-discipline."** The spiritual you is powerful, loving and self-disciplined! It's up to us to keep this spiritual mindset when we pray. (Actually this should be our mindset in whatever we are doing!) Our pray life should be based on **"power"** and **"love."** The **"self-discipline"** part is the fact that we discipline ourselves to pray rather than worry, talk about the problem or even just plain forget to pray.

Ephesians 6:18 also says to **"pray... with all kinds of prayers".** We know that prayer means to talk to God, our Father. We've spoken about praise, thanksgiving and requests, but there is another kind of prayer we haven't covered and that is speaking in tongues.

Speaking in Tongues

Many Christians know little about this kind of prayer. Some find it strange and others believe that it was only for the 1st century church. One thing I know is... it's in the bible and explained rather clearly.

> **"For anyone who speaks in tongues does not speak to men but to God. Indeed, no one understands him; he utters mysteries with his spirit."**
> I Corinthians 14:2

Notice it says that when you speak in tongues you are speaking to God, which is what prayer is. I Corinthians 14:14 Apostle Paul goes on to say: **"For if I pray in a tongue, my spirit prays but my mind is unfruitful. So what shall I do? I will pray with my spirit, but I will also pray with my mind; I will sing with my spirit but I will also sing with my mind. If you are praising God with your spirit, how can one who finds himself among those who do not understand say "Amen" to your thanksgiving, since he does not know what you are saying? You may be giving thanks well enough, but the other man is not edified."**

It's pretty obvious to note that **"speaking in tongues"** is for our private prayer life. It's a language that we don't even know. What we do know is that it's praising God. It's giving thanks well.

The very first time people received the gift of Holy Spirit on the day of Pentecost they spoke in tongues. **"All of them were filled with the Holy Spirit and began to speak with other tongues as the Spirit enabled them."** Acts 2:4

The first record of non-Jews, gentiles, receiving the Holy Spirit tells us that they also spoke in tongues. **"The circumcised believers who had come with Peter were astonished that the gift of the Holy Spirit had been poured out even on the Gentiles. For they heard them speaking in tongues and praising God."** Acts 10:45-46   One very significant benefit of speaking in tongues that we can note from this verse is that when you or anyone you know speaks in tongues you can be sure that you (or they) are saved because they have received the gift of the Holy Spirit. Of course, the other major benefit is that we are praising God. Acts 2:11 says, **"...declaring the wonders of God."**   Remember, we enter His presence with praise!

Speaking in tongues, praying in the spirit, is definitely helpful in the battle. Sometimes we don't know what to pray for or we spiritually sense something very heavy in the air around us. Speaking in tongues quietly to God, words He has authored, opens the door for His power to work through us. I Corinthians 14:4 tells us that speaking in tongues edifies us. To edify means to build up, to empower. Something every soldier needs!

Some of you reading this who don't speak in tongues might be wondering... Okay, well how can I? It's pretty simple. I still remember the first time I spoke in tongues. I was 20 years old. I was told that to speak any language, you need to open your mouth and move your lips. Well, that's... obvious! Then I was told to speak in tongues you also needed to do the same thing. I closed my eyes and asked God to help me. Then I started to move my mouth and lips and make a noise. A word came out! Not one that I knew the meaning to! Then I moved my mouth again and pushed out another word then another and another. That's it! It is very simple. I've been speaking and singing in tongues in my private prayer life ever since. Like Apostle Paul, I too can say **"I thank God that I speak in tongues..."** 1 Corinthians 14:18

Be An Alert Prayer Warrior

Again speaking in tongues is one of **"all the kinds of prayers"** we are to pray. The whole point of this verse is to pray! The last half of Ephesians 6:18 says: **"With this in mind, be alert and always keep on praying for all the saints."** Notice it says: **"Be alert."** Any soldier knows that alertness is very important when you are in a battle. When we notice, because we are alert, any form of attack - we pray. It doesn't matter if the battle is in our own homes or an attack against believers across the world. We are called to pray for **"all the saints."** That seems massive, but remember who we are praying to. The God who created each and every person on this earth! **"With God all things are possible."** Matthew 19:26

The choice is up to us to use this armor! When we do we are... dangerous to the evil forces that are trying to wreck havoc in this world. So with that in mind, **"keep on praying for all the saints."** Including yourself!

Conclusion

Stand Your Ground!

"Therefore put on the full armor of God, so that when the day of evil comes, you may be able to stand your ground, and after you have done everything, to stand."
Ephesians 6:13

The purpose of this book was to help you and me **"be strong in the Lord and the power of HIS might."** Why? So we could be powerful warriors, who wreak havoc against our enemy's schemes. As you have read, we have been given the armor and the privilege to do this. It's up to us to make the choice to put on this armor each and everyday.

Grab the **"belt of truth"** and cinch it tight. Make it a habit to study God's Word daily so you know it, think it and live it out.

Have the **"breastplate of righteousness"** in place. Remember our Lord Jesus Christ paid the price for you to shine bright as a righteous child of God. He is the atoning sacrifice for our sins. Forgiveness is always available. Don't allow condemnation or self-righteousness get in the way of you living out your calling as an instrument of righteousness.

Stand firmly, always prepared because you are wearing the **footwear of peace**. It's your choice to live in peace, no matter what's going on around you. You can choose to stand unified with God in Christ. A peacemaker for others and yourself!

Take up the **"shield of faith,"** your extinguisher that puts out every flaming arrow from the evil one. You can always approach the throne of grace with confidence: the faith to ask Jesus for help knowing He's there for you. Knowing that through this faith in Jesus you are an overcomer!

Wear your **"helmet of salvation"** for all to see. Live your life in light of eternity. Rejoice continually in the fact that you are saved and one day will meet the Lord in the air. That you will be with Him forever! Also, that He has rewards waiting for any of us who lived for Him.

Be offensive! Gentle with people but on the offense against evil. Grab your **"sword of the spirit"** and slash every argument and pretension that sets itself up against the truth. Speak what God's Word says, the truth, to your heart and to the hearts of those who are in prison by the lies they believe. Break open those prison doors with the truth that sets us free!

"Pray!" Pray for God's will to be done on earth. Pray continually because your prayers are powerful and effective to defeat the devil's schemes.

You've been given armor – the armor of God, which was paid for by His Son, our Lord and Savior, Jesus Christ. You have the ability each and every moment of the day to be powerfully, powerful!

Decide to wear your armor. When you do you will be **STANDING STRONG IN THE POWER OF <u>HIS</u> MIGHT!**

Made in the USA
Charleston, SC
29 April 2015